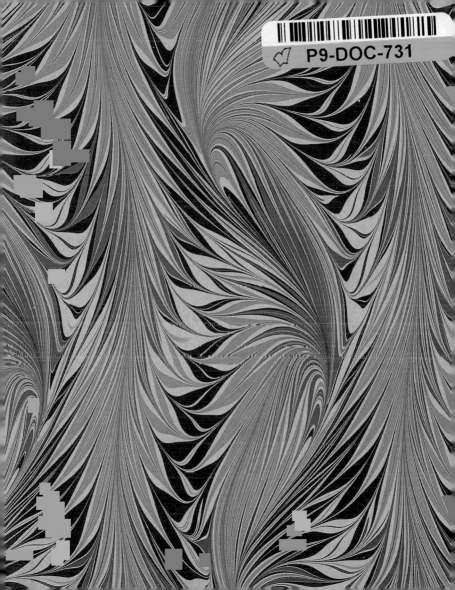

THE GARDEN
GATE

THE LIBRARY *of* GARDEN DETAIL

THE GARDEN
GATE

ROSEMARY VEREY

Simon and Schuster

New York   London   Toronto   Sydney   Tokyo   Singapore

Simon and Schuster

Simon & Schuster Building

Rockefeller Center

1230 Avenue of the Americas

New York, New York 10020

First published in Great Britain in 1991 by
Pavilion Books Limited

196 Shaftesbury Avenue, London WC2H 8JL

Designed by Paul Burcher

Printed and bound in Italy by L.E.G.O., Vicenza

Library of Congress Cataloguing in Publication Data

Verey, Rosemary.
    The garden gate/Rosemary Verey.
        p. cm.—(The Library of garden detail)
        "First published in Great Britain in 1991 by Pavilion Books
    Limited"—T.p. verso.
        ISBN 0-671-74405-4
        1. Gates   2. Garden structures   I. Title   II. Series
    TH4965.V47   1991
    717—dc20

                                    91-9545
                                    CIP

10   9   8   7   6   5   4   3   2   1

Beverly Fawdre

CONTENTS

❦

6

ℐNTRODUCTION

ℊATES HAVE MANY PURPOSES — PRACTICAL, ROMANTIC AND ornamental. Once we had a wooden round-slatted white gate at the bottom of our back stairs, and my young nephew, son of a Scottish farmer, asked knowledgeably if it was to keep the hoggets (young sheep) out. 'No,' I told him, 'it is only to stop our young whippets from going upstairs.' Later it became the gate into our kitchen garden, where it had the practical use of keeping the rabbits out, and was also ornamental, the straight slats echoing the direction of the straight path beyond.

7

As Tennyson reminds us, gates may play a romantic role:

Come into the garden, Maud,

I am here at the gate alone;

And the woodbine spices are wafted abroad,

And the musk of the rose is blown.

Was Tennyson's young lover, I wonder, leaning wistfully over a friendly wooden gate, rather like mine, with his elbows resting comfortably on the topmost rail, relaxed and happy? Somehow I think it was one of those gates beloved of Victorian painters, set in a mellow stone wall, framed with honeysuckle on one side and roses on the other, the scent wafting romantically on the air so that when the lovers were reunited their embraces were sweet.

Historians will tell you that the Old English word 'gaet' meant an opening in a city wall with a movable barrier – sometimes a drawbridge or portcullis to bar the way. Just think of the later Northgate, Southgate, Westgate and Eastgates protecting the city of Gloucester.

In more rural settings, illustrations in *The Romance of the Rose*, c.1475, show trellis fences and arched gates made of sawn wood called carpenters' work. A hundred years later Thomas Hill, in *The Gardener's Labyrinth* of 1577, has woodcuts of gardens which are decorative and full of information. These gardens are enclosed by a wall or fence,

1. *This solid gate is made of oak of fine craftsmanship and design; the silvery brown wood has mellowed beautifully and merges wonderfully into the Cotswold stone.*

with a solid wooden gate strapped and bolted with strong ironwork. One is set into a vine-covered arch and surround and set into a brick wall. Both have heavy locks – a wise precaution, for as the Clown sings in *Twelfth Night*, 'Gainst knaves and thieves men shut their gates'. The frontispiece of Ralph Austen's *A Treatise on Fruit Trees* of 1653 also shows 'a garden inclosed', with two handsome wooden gates set into a high brick wall; one has a broken pediment with a central urn and the other two pillars surmounted by balls.

In *Systema Horti-culturae* (1677), John Worlidge shows for one garden design a conventional solid wooden gate with a pediment, and adds another design with a fence and gate made of palisades with brick pillars; the gate echoes the fence. 'These open Fences are made of Board of about three or four inches broad, and three or four foot long, either nailed to, or let thorow two Rails, with head cut either round or like a Lance, and painted white ... But the best material to make these Pallisades withal is Iron, so framed as are the Iron Balconies in London.'

In 1697 Leonard Meager, as the frontispiece of his book *New Art of Gardening*, shows a garden divided into different compartments by architectural features – walls, balustrades and gateways. In his illustrations the bottom of the gate is solid and the wooden palings of the top, and the fence, corresponds with a low brick wall and brick pillars.

10

After the sombre gardening days of the Common-
wealth, the pleasure garden once more became important
with the restoration of the monarchy and the influence of
the continent. The French Huguenot, Jean Tijou, came to

2. *These magnificent gates at Hampton Court
Palace are the work of Huguenot Jean Tijou. The
detail of his repoussé work is delicate and was
much copied by other artists.*

11

England, where he worked for William and Mary at
Hampton Court, making the exquisite ironwork gates and
panels leading from the formal parterre garden to the
avenues of the *patte d'oie*. His technique was to hammer and

shape flat sheets of metal into decorative relief; then the blacksmith would have welded them by heating them to a bright red heat and forcing them together. The wrought-iron motifs for this repoussé work included masks, eagle heads, monograms and crests, acanthus and bay leaves, often on the overthrows above the gates.

Tijou's work had an important influence on other craftsmen; there were a number of smiths whose names are associated with gardens of this period. At the turn of the century Robert Bakewell of Derby was working at Melbourne and Thomas Robinson of London making the exquisite gates and screen, 130ft (40m) long, at New College, Oxford; and in 1719 the Welsh brothers Robert and Thomas Davies of Wrexham were creating the wonderful iron gates and clairvoyée at Chirk Castle. Probably they had studied Tijou's book, published in 1700, for their work resembles his.

These elaborate and beautiful gates suited the formal gardens of the period with their parterres and patterns, but

12

fashion was changing and planting round the big houses was swept away. Trees in the parkland became the all-important feature, and visitors arriving in their carriages up long drives viewed the carefully landscaped scene as they approached the house. Livestock were part of this idyllic scene, so gates must be kept closed – grand and imposing gates as befitted a mansion. A gatehouse – often two – was essential, for it was the gate-keeper's duty to be constantly on the alert for visitors and open the gates at the approach of their carriages. In 1726 James Gibbs designed at the new western entrance to Stowe park the Boycott Lodges, in the form of rus-

3. *The wrought-iron screen and overthrow re-erected at the end of the canal at Erddig is thought to have been made by Robert Davies of Wrexham in the 1720s.*

13

ticated cubes with tall pedimented arches. These lodges were superseded when Vincenzo Valdre's twin Buckingham Lodges were erected at the entrance to the Grand Avenue, and were left simply as features in the landscape. To me the most spectacular park lodge is Worcester Lodge, designed by William Kent in 1746 to face the north façade of

4. *This clairvoyée was made wide enough to view the lime avenue beyond. It is set into massive stone piers topped by gigantic urns, and the whole concept has perfect proportions in the context of the landscape.*

Badminton House at the end of a three-mile drive.

In the Regency period ironwork verandahs and porches were built, with ironwork gates leading into the newly

14

restored flower gardens. Designed in elegant patterns, thankfully much of this beautiful work has survived. Then the use of cast iron for garden ornaments and for gates and railings became fashionable, and for a time it replaced the more delicate wrought iron.

At this point we should clarify as simply as possible the terms wrought and cast iron. Wrought iron is a refined form from which oxygen and other impurities have been removed. It can be hammered, squeezed or rolled into shape, and when two pieces are heated intensively and forced together, they will weld. The metal is good at resisting corrosion. By the mid-nineteenth century a substitute had been found for wrought iron – mild steel, a metal chemically akin to wrought iron but physically different. It can be worked by forging and rolling in the same manner as wrought iron and can be welded easily. Since World War I, gates and railings have been made of this metal, but corrosion has arisen, and today all so-called wrought-iron gates are actually made of mild steel.

16

5. *A well designed gateway in an American garden. The gate has diamond shapes and a sunray pattern with ironwork pillars ornamented with circles and diamonds — all is in keeping with the neo-Georgian house.*

By the mid-nineteenth century cast iron was also increasingly used. Easier to produce than wrought iron, it is made by melting iron ore in a furnace and running the molten iron into shaped moulds; but it cannot be rolled and forged. Cast-iron patterns can be beautiful, especially when the artist recognizes that it is inevitably heavier and more solid in character.

As long as we have horses to be shod, there will always be village blacksmiths, many of them artists able to make fine iron gates to their own design. The Arts and Crafts movement encouraged the craft of ironwork, using their own distinctive designs. Wrought iron, especially when it is well decorated, is expensive, but simpler patterns with delicate bar work can be beautiful and are often not as costly as one might imagine.

Start thinking about and taking notice of gates – their structure, the materials they are made from, their purpose, their colour, their durability. Are they inviting; do they add dignity, strength and satisfaction; or do they give you an urge to remove them? All these questions will reverberate in your mind and you will observe features with new eyes. At Hutton-in-the-Forest in Cumbria I noticed that the double gates had a wooden framework, the base is designed on the wheel pattern with iron bars above, and the gate piers are of solid stone; so here you have three elements combined – stone, wood and iron. There is no overthrow and the piers are wide enough to allow a carriage and pair to drive through into the forecourt and right up to the front door.

18

The late seventeenth-century moated house, Groombridge Place in Kent, has imposing stone piers surmounted by stone pineapples. Again this gate is an early example of combining a wooden frame with iron bars, but on each side it also has niches which, unusually, face each other. Sometimes grand entrance gates were hung directly on to stone gate piers, sometimes on to metal piers positioned just inside the opening, so giving a wider span in total. This is the case with the Lion Gates at Hampton Court, and in addition they have an iron panel each side with a surrounding frame on which the twin gates hang, and above all this an elaborate overthrow. The wonderful crafts-

26. *The design of this pretty, rather conventional iron gate shows up well against the pale background of the road and complements the planting of dark leaves of* Prunus cerasifera *'Pissardii'.*

manship of these gates with their many different motifs, should be studied, but to me the huge and imposing pillars carrying the lion couchant seem overwhelming companions to the beautiful and delicate ironwork. The grand yet austere style of the eighteenth-century iron gates at Penshurst Place in Kent by contrast are in good proportion, the brick piers with stone balls on finials and the design of the overthrow combining perfectly with the design within the gate. These imposing gateways certainly may be an inspiration to us, but so too may far smaller and more modest ones be. It is important to look and always to analyse.

20

When it comes to designing your own front gate, you must first consider the situation: what are the qualities you will be looking for? The gates must open easily but not be difficult to shut. Will they open inwards or outwards? They must be attractive and solid enough to keep out your neighbour's dog and cat and blowing leaves and litter. Gates are symbolic: they either discourage or encourage you to enter. A solid wooden gate, made like a door with a difficult handle to turn, will cause you to wonder if you are wanted on the other side, but a prettily designed wooden gate, solid

67. *Just as dramatic is this solid wooden gate with its round porthole allowing an enticing view through into the woodland beyond but made safe from intruders by its wrought ironwork.*

at the base and with a see-through pattern above, can be intriguing and arouse your curiosity. It may be only a half-gate, 3ft 6in high (1.2m), one you can lean over – in fact Maud's gate.

Old cottages and small town houses are probably best with wooden slatted gates, kept to the natural wood or painted to match the window frames and front door. Their style must suit the building. In contrast, the manor house or grander town house should have a more ornate design, wrought-iron with a pattern which fits the date of the house or cast-iron if it is high Victorian.

8. *It is sometimes sad to obscure the view out of the garden, and here the gate invites you to step out into the countryside. It is simple in design, set between Cotswold stone monoliths.*

Then you can use your imagination to create new places for gates inside your garden – you may well discover strategic spots where one will undoubtedly add a touch of elegance or romance, or simply an invitation to explore further. Pleasure garden and kitchen garden gates should be solid enough to keep out the cold wind and the rabbits, but need not be dull: the pattern can be dense, or their lower half solid with a decorated design above. You could include a gate where you have an archway, or add one at the top of a slope or to emphasize two different parts of the garden. If you have a boundary hedge or wall, there is nothing to stop you putting in a gate even if the adjoining land is not yours, and this will give you a feeling of extended ownership, not to mention an extra vista.

When choosing the colour for your gate, remember that a lighter colour – white or cream – can be used against a dark background but a dark colour is more appropriate if it is seen against the sky or distant fields or parkland. It will stand out in silhouette, and when the sun is low will cast its own shadow on the ground. Perhaps it is pure convention, but I do not like the idea of a brightly coloured iron gate: keep the colour cool and blending, and remember that it will last for years if you do not allow it to rust. A subtle gilding of ornamental detail on black gates adds a touch of grandeur, but must not be overdone. There is so much green in nature that I believe it is the last colour to choose for gates and railings. A deep blue can blend in well, especially if it is associated with water; it is hard to choose a better colour than black.

If you crave for colour with a difference, choose wood instead of iron. Red, yellow and pale blue-green are colours associated with Chinese Chippendale patterns. Charles Paget Wade at Snowshill and Lawrence Johnston at nearby Hidcote in Gloucestershire had their special Hidcote blue. While white looks well on bright days and in countries abroad where the light is intense, it can sometimes stand out too starkly in our English climate, especially if the gate is large and solid.

At the front of old country cottages however, where the hedge has grown massive, forming a screen, and the garden behind is filled with an abundance of flowers, a small white wicket gate adds charm and fits the scene perfectly. A

9. *The way from cottage garden to lawn and woodland is well expressed by this natural coloured wooden gate. You are led on by the lines of nepeta and pair of standard* Rosa *'Nozomi' surrounded by scented dianthus.*

white-painted gate on a modern town house may be too glaring, calling out to passers-by – better perhaps to have a more mellow colour, one which will blend in with its surroundings. In stone country this can be grey with a touch of gold in it to lift and enliven it, making it veer towards a more subtle honey colour. In brick country it is important to keep away from yellows – here it is better to concentrate on a darker, more neutral colour, or simply keep to natural wood.

The moment will come when you start to be critical about the overgrowth of climbers obscuring or even obliterating a beautiful gateway. It can easily happen and is a prudent reminder that every area of the garden should be looked at questioningly. Remember that every addition must be an improvement, not a distraction. You do not want to hide your pretty ironwork, so garland it with a rose or clematis which will emphasize its beauty; but a wooden gateway well draped with climbers – ivy and honeysuckle – becomes romantic and adds mystery.

$\mathcal{G}$RAND $\mathcal{J}$RON

10. *This is one of my favourite gates, perfect for its position and design. Placed at the top of a garden on three levels, a flight of steps leads up to imposing gates with posts and finials, all in perfect proportion.*

28

11. *The beautiful wrought-iron gates are set between square Cotswold*
stone pillars surmounted by stone balls. The decoration is in flowing
neo-classical style, strongly silhouetted against the sky. The wall is so low
that it makes the pillars feel isolated.

12. *The importance of shadows and evening light becomes clear seeing this gate with its unusually designed overthrow. However I think that the proportions would be improved either without the balls and their supports, or with the pillars reduced in size.*

30

13. *These elegant iron gates piercing the*
fifteenth-century brick wall at Hatfield House
show the way from the wilderness into the scented
garden. The stone balls were placed there by the
present Lady Salisbury.

14. *This gateway in a lovely old brick wall has a light and airy quality and the vertical bars allow the visitor to see down the twin herbaceous borders to the mellow brick house. The overthrow is flowing yet simple.*

32

15. *The grand stonework into which this wrought-iron gate is set could have some of the foliage clipped back to reveal the curved shape of the wall, echoing the arch at the top of the gate.*

SMALL IRON

16. *Why not consider a lower gate — especially if there is luxuriant growth all around? Here the black iron gate is framed by a clipped yew hedge and an arched wall. But the drama is increased by the snowfall, making the ironwork design stand out.*

34

17. *Garden walls create wonderful opportunities for iron gates –*
transparent gates through which you have a tantalizing view towards the
garden beyond. They can make a bold statement, as in this Irish garden
where the Gothic arches reflect the pointed stone arch.

18. *Another Irish gate I remember, because of its impeccable craftsmanship, is set into a stone wall at Mount Congreve; it was made for Ambrose Congreve, the present owner and creator of the garden.*

19. *By contrast, and something of an understatement, is the romantic,
probably little-used gate in a red brick wall, overhung by a lime tree and
the shade-loving climber* Hydrangea petiolaris. *It has an atmosphere
of love, not neglect.*

20. (below left) *An old wrought-iron gate set into a brick wall at*
Newby Hall has rounded clipped columns of yew on each side. Luxuriant
Clematis armandii *is established securely under the brick wall.*

37

21. (above right) *A gateway designed by Sir Edwin Lutyens with*
characteristic stonework frames a heavy iron gate. Its austere effect would
be spoilt by a cloak of foliage or flowers, but the large leaves of the fig
tree are strong enough to hold their own.

22. This gateway benefits from its embellishment of Clematis *'Jackmanii Superba'. However the gate, with its heavy bars, together with its surround of dressed Cotswold stone, is beautiful in its own right.*

23. *The evening sun highlights the S-motif pattern on this gate made in the 1960s at Barnsley House. The morning sun casts a reflection of the pattern of the gate on the stone path beyond.*

40

24/25. *Two satisfactory white-painted, cast-iron gates giving a cottage garden effect. The red brick piers with simple pots (left) has* Rosa *'Nevada' arching loosely but gracefully over them. The closed gate (right) has an arched framework to support the pink rambler rose; deep pink hollyhocks arch up also, and the box edging leading you up to the gate is in keeping with the straight, upright bars.*

26. *The lightness of this three-quarter height gate matches its frame of feathery evergreens. The S-motif pattern is cleverly used to create a minimal barrier with a clear and inviting view of the garden beyond.*

27. *These attractive gates in Scotland were made in the late nineteenth century. Yew trees flank its stone pillars, and the gate connects the rhododendron avenue with the garden round the house.*

28. *Cranborne Manor is the romantic setting for a pair of elegant wrought-iron gates. The oak pillars are unusually tall and have aged to a beautiful silvery grey.*

44

29. *An interestingly designed modern gate in the remarkable garden created by the late Robin Spencer at York Gate, near Leeds. The various spirals are in keeping with the whole garden.*

30. *A pair of peacock gates in the sundial garden at Jenkyns Place was made especially for Mr and Mrs Gerald Coke in the 1950s by their local blacksmith. This unusually beautiful design fits perfectly into their garden.*

31. *The blue-purple of* Clematis durandii *makes a perfectly blending picture with the blue of the cast-iron gates.*

46

32. Another well-thought-out entrance gate leading from the road, the pattern of the ironwork echoing the stone balls. The charm of the scene lies in the luxuriant plants and the view through the open front door to the garden beyond.

ᗯHITE ᗯOOD

33. *An Australian fence in the main street in Ballarat, Victoria, a town which sprang up in the 1880s, as a result of the gold rush. The whole shape of this gate and fence, with its panels like a folded-out screen, is pleasing and attracts your attention.*

48

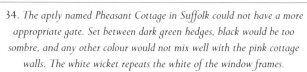

34. *The aptly named* Pheasant Cottage *in* Suffolk *could not have a more appropriate gate. Set between dark green hedges, black would be too sombre, and any other colour would not mix well with the pink cottage walls. The white wicket repeats the white of the window frames.*

35. *White windows, a white front door and a white porch must have a white gate. All are in keeping with the characterful cottage — the only feature lacking is the owner in her white apron.*

36. *The pattern of this gate at Trerice in Cornwall is probably contemporary with its Elizabethan house. The black ironwork on the white wood gives it strength and interest, and I like the height of the piers and their balancing balls and the way the wall rises as it joins the piers.*

37. *This 'harvest gate' gives an immediate rustic air. It is an original
idea successfully carried out with hayforks, garden rakes, an old scythe
and two sickles.*

52

38/39. In Williamsburg, Virginia, the gardens, as well as the buildings, have been faithfully restored to the Colonial fashion of the early eighteenth century. These simple white picket fences have been re-erected in their original positions by excavating to find the position and size of the old post holes.

40. *This handsome wooden gate was found in the attic at Painswick House by Lord Dickinson. Its Chinese-influenced patterns and its acute-angled trelliswork make it difficult to repair, but the iron hinges and stays will take the strain of the gate itself.*

41. *With the strong sunshine, white gates and fences become an integral part of this American garden. A carpenter's work tunnel leads through into the garden, and has its arch effect repeated at the end of the brick path – an idea carried on in the United States from Colonial times.*

42. *An ornamental wooden fence and gate make the garden boundary. The alternating long and short bars, reminiscent of organ pipes, give a feeling of rhythm. All make you aware that you are entering no ordinary American garden.*

56

43. *Harvey Ladew, a fox-hunting man, made his
famous topiary garden at Monkton in Maryland.
Here the clipped boxwood huntsman and his horse
are leaping the white field gate; the fox and
hounds are ahead.*

COLOURED
WOOD

44. *This almost solid gate makes a clear statement. It marks the way between two clipped hornbeam hedges and the wooden slats have become the colour of the hornbeam branches in winter.*

45. *In a Cotswold garden this wooden Chinese Chippendale gate is painted the palest blue-green. The spikes of iris leaves echo the pattern of the gate slats and complement their colour.* Clematis *'Gravetye Beauty' and the rampant rose 'Bobby James' create a romantic setting for the half-hidden gateway.*

46. *The garden at Great Dixter is remarkable both for its inspired planting by Christopher Lloyd and its architectural layout. There is such a wealth of inspiration for the visitor that no smaller, less obvious features should be overlooked. The Lutyens-designed gate is a gem – take note of its details.*

47. *If your garden gate leads directly onto a busy road, you may want it to be made of solid wood. Once inside you have a twofold welcome. The slightly curved top of the gate adds interest, and is protected by a brick drip mould.*

48. *A unique gate at Dumbarton Oaks in Washington DC, the garden designed by Beatrice Farrand early this century for Mr and Mrs Bliss. The low gate is not a visual barrier: visitors are intended to see beyond. Its whole design is unique in the combination of wood, iron and stone.*

SOURCES

Some UK Addresses

Cannock Gates
Dept HG
Hawks Green Industrial Estate
Martindale
Cannock
Staffordshire
WS11 2XT
Telephone: (0543) 462500

Britannia
5 Normandy Street
Alton
Hampshire
GU34 1DD
Telephone: (0420) 84427

Barnsley House GDF
Barnsley House
Cirencester
Gloucestershire, GL7 5EE
Telephone: (0285) 74561

Some US Addresses

Cassidy Brothers Forge Inc.
US Route 1
Rowley, MA 01969-1796
Telephone: (617) 948-7611

International Terracotta Inc.
690 North Robertson Boulevard
Los Angeles, CA 90069-5088
Telephone: (213) 657-3752

Iron Fence Co.
PO Box 467
Auburn, IN 46706
Telephone: (219) 925-4264

Robinson Iron
Robinson Road
Alexander City, AL 35010
Telephone: (205) 329-8486

Vintage Gazebos
Dept 367
513 South Adams
Fredericksburg, TX 78624
Telephone: (512) 997-9513

Walpole Woodworkers
767 East St
Walpole, MA 02081
Telephone: (617) 668-2800

PICTURE CREDITS

The Publisher thanks the following photographers and
organizations for their kind permission to reproduce photographs
in this book.
Owners and designers of gardens are credited where known.
Photographers appear in bold type.

Title page. **Derek Fell**; private garden, USA
page 6. **Andrew Lawson**; Alderley Grange, Gloucestershire
Picture No 1 **Jerry Harpur**; Ablington Manor
Picture No 2 **Hugh Palmer**; Hampton Court, Surrey
Picture No 3 **Eric Crichton**; The National Trust, Erddig, Clwyd
Picture No 4 **Eric Crichton**; The National Trust, Ham House, Surrey
Picture No 5 **Derek Fell**; private garden, USA
Picture No 6 **Georges Lévêque**; Coates Manor, Fittleworth, Pulborough, West Sussex
Picture No 7 **Derek Fell**; private garden, USA
Picture No 8 **Georges Lévêque**; The National Trust, Snowshill Manor, Gloucestershire
Picture No 9 **Eric Crichton**; Mrs J. Foulsham, Vale End, Surrey
Picture No 10 **Hugh Palmer**; Château de Brécy, France
Picture No 11 **Hugh Palmer**; Abbotswood, Stow-on-the-Wold, Gloucestershire
Picture No 12 **Eric Crichton**; The National Trust, Erddig, Clwyd
Picture No 13 **Eric Crichton**; The National Trust, Ham House, Surrey
Picture No 14 **Georges Lévêque**; Bramdean House, Near Alresford, Hampshire
Picture No 15 **Georges Lévêque**; Garinish Island, County Cork, Ireland
Picture No 16 **S + O Mathews**; private garden, Godstone, Surrey
Picture No 17 **Georges Lévêque**; Mrs B. Farquhar, County Tipperary, Ireland
Picture No 18 **Georges Lévêque**; Mount Congreve, near Waterford, Ireland
Picture No 19 **Georges Lévêque**; private garden, Great Britain
Picture No 20 **Eric Crichton**; R.E.J. Compton, Newby Hall, Yorkshire
Picture No 21 **Eric Crichton**; Devon Fire Brigade, Hestercombe, Somerset
Picture No 22 **Andrew Lawson**; The Ivy House, Charlbury, Oxfordshire
Picture No 23 **Andrew Lawson**; Mrs Rosemary Verey, Barnsley House, Gloucestershire

63

Picture No 24 **Eric Crichton**; Mrs P. Sinclair, Lime Tree Cottage, Surrey
Picture No 25 **Jerry Harpur**; House of Pitmuies, Guthrie, Tayside, Scotland
Picture No 26 **Eric Crichton**; Mrs G. D. Gough, Trevi Gardens, Hartpury, Gloucestershire
Picture No 27 **Jerry Harpur**; Mellerstain, Gordon, Etterick, Borders, Scotland
Picture No 28 **Jerry Harpur**; Cranborne Manor Gardens, Dorset
Picture No 29 **Eric Crichton**; Mrs S. Spencer, York Gate, Leeds, Yorkshire
Picture No 30 **Georges Lévêque**; Jenkyn Place, Bentley, Hampshire
Picture No 31 **Georges Lévêque**; Mrs Rosemary Verey, Barnsley House, Gloucestershire
Picture No 32 **Hugh Palmer**; Stone Cottage, Hambleton, Oakham, Leicestershire
Picture No 33 **Jerry Harpur**; Ballarat, Victoria, Australia
Picture No 34 **Andrew Lawson**; Pheasant Cottage, Horringer, Suffolk
Picture No 35 **Eric Crichton**; Great Tew, Oxfordshire
Picture No 36 **Hugh Palmer**; The National Trust, Trerice, Cornwall
Picture No 37 **Eric Crichton**; The Harvest Gate, Wormborne, Wodehouse
Picture No 38 **Hugh Palmer**; private garden, Williamsburg, VA, USA
Picture No 39 **Hugh Palmer**; private garden, Williamsburg, VA, USA
Picture No 40 **Hugh Palmer**; The National Trust, Painswick, Gloucestershire
Picture No 41 **Jerry Harpur**; Bruce Wells (designer), New York, USA
Picture No 42 **Derek Fell**; private garden, USA
Picture No 43 **Derek Fell**; Ladew garden, Monkton, Maryland, MA, USA
Picture No 44 **Georges Lévêque**; Jacques Wirtz, Schoten, Belgium
Picture No 45 **Georges Lévêque**; Bampton Manor, Oxfordshire
Picture No 46 **S + O Mathews**; Great Dixter, Northiam, East Sussex
Picture No 47 **Georges Lévêque**; Tudor Hotel, Godalming, Surrey
Picture No 48 **Hugh Palmer**; Dumbarton Oaks, Washington DC, USA